An Autistic Perspective

Death, Dying and Loss

FIRST EDITION

Dan Jones

Connect with Dan Jones: www.ALT-Solutions.org

First Edition 2017

Published by Dan Jones

Copyright © Daniel Jones 2017

Lulu Publishing Edition

Daniel Jones asserts the moral right to be identified as the author of this work

All rights reserved. No part of this publication may be reproduced, stored in a retrieval system, or transmitted, in any form or by any means, electronic, mechanical, photocopying, recording, or otherwise, without the prior written permission of the publishers or author.

ISBN 978-0-244-31407-1

Twitter: @AuthorDanJones

Table of Contents

CHAPTER ONE *Introduction* 1

CHAPTER TWO *Loss* 5

CHAPTER THREE *Dying & Death* 23

CHAPTER FOUR *Conclusion* 47

CHAPTER ONE

Introduction

The topics of death, dying and loss have interested me since I was a young child. From early on in my life I noticed that people seemed to be uncomfortable talking about these subjects. People would tell me it was morbid, it upset them, or they didn't want to think about it. To me, though, it was interesting. It is a part of life that you can't escape. Death, dying and loss will happen to everyone.

After I wrote *Look Into My Eyes*, a book about my experiences growing up and living with autism spectrum disorder, I realised the topics of death and dying weren't really focused on at all. The book had helpful tips and strategies for parents, carers, teachers, friends and employers of those with autism spectrum disorder, and for those who have autism. It also had a chapter by my wife about what it is like to be in a relationship with someone with autism.

It may seem odd that I even considered how these topics weren't focused on, and you may be wondering why I would notice this. When I first started thinking about writing *Look Into My Eyes*, it was following the death of my dad, after learning that he had recognised that I was different as a young child. This awareness contributed to me seeking an autism spectrum disorder diagnosis and consequently my decision to write a book to help me gain greater insight about myself, whilst simultaneously helping others gain an insight into what it is like to be autistic. In preparation for writing my book, I created a mind map focusing on different life stages, and for each life stage I included the struggles and traits I'd had and how I'd coped. I wanted the book to be helpful to those who interact with people with autism spectrum disorder, and helpful for the people with autism spectrum disorder too.

About six months after the original book was published, I decided to write a second edition. I had been giving talks about my experiences with autism and was regularly asked about what it was like for my wife to be in a relationship with someone with autism. People wanted to know the challenges and positive aspects, and how we both coped and managed to maintain a relationship. This became a line of questioning I would be asked at all the talks I gave. It became something that a couple of national newspapers and magazines also wanted to cover, and I realised I hadn't really covered it in detail in my book, especially not from the non-autistic partner's perspective. This led me to wonder what else was missing from my book.

Another thing people requested were all the various tips and strategies I shared throughout the book to be in a single place, perhaps all in a chapter of their own, and people asked if I could expand on some of the ideas I shared from my personal and professional experiences, so I wrote another title, *Asperger's Syndrome: Tips and Strategies*, to cover all the various tips and strategies in a single volume. I also noticed in everyday life that things would happen - I would think about something in a specific way, or would have certain reactions to things - and at those times I would realise that I hadn't included anything about them in my book, despite them sometimes occurring even on a daily basis. This is one of the difficulties with sitting somewhere quiet and 'safe' when I am writing - it is very hard to connect with my experiences from other times of my life, sometimes even remembering things from earlier in the same day. It's not like I'd reacted with anxiety or anger in a situation and thought 'I had better get a notepad out and jot that down to remind myself to include it in my book', because in those moments I was too busy dealing with the situation.

In all of my talks, no-one had asked about my views on death, dying, or loss, so I didn't think about it as something missing, or as something people may be interested in. It wasn't until my granddad died in August 2016, when people started asking if I was okay and telling me it must be so upsetting, and how sad they felt for me, that I realised I didn't think about my granddad's death in this way. I then made an off-the-cuff comment about the suffering my dad went through as he died and, again, had the reaction that it must have been so difficult. It was only then that I started to process how I think about death, dying and loss, and how most others seem to process these; I realised it could be interesting to people to gain insight into how my mind works with these things. I've had people say that they wish they processed things more like how I do, so perhaps some of this will be of help to people in how they can manage death, dying and loss.

It is important to note that, although I am writing about my own autistic perspective on death, dying and loss, this perspective won't be shared by all with autism. Everyone, autistic and non-autistic, thinks differently. I think there are some similarities that most people with autism will recognise, but they may not share how certain traits express for me personally. Hopefully what I share here will also be of use to parents and carers of those with autism, offering some insight into the mind of those with autism and helping to explain behaviours they may see, as well as some ideas about how best to approach the subjects of death, dying and loss.

Although the title is ordered 'death, dying and loss', I will cover these three areas in the opposite order. For a title, I felt that they sounded better in this order, but through this book I will be covering loss in one chapter and then dying and death in another chapter, because this is a more natural order. We experience various forms of loss throughout our lives from birth and, as we become aware of our mortality, we start to think about aging and dying; likewise, we often experience people going through a period of dying before death.

In the chapter on loss, the main focus is on relationship breakups and on transitions we face, like transitioning from one school to another, or from one job to another, or from living at home to independent living. Although death involves loss, and dying involves the awareness that loss will be inevitable, I have tried to keep these areas distinct and within their own chapter. In the chapter about dying and death I share about my experiences of people dying and the positive and negative aspects of my way of being in relation to those who are dying; on death, I share about my experiences of death, and how I respond to the death of loved ones.

My hope is that, by going into detail in an honest and frank way, this will help to give insight into the autistic mind, and how my mind processes these areas of life. Throughout the chapters I will share some tips and ideas that parents, carers, partners or friends can do to help the autistic individual, and to understand them and interact with them in a way that respects their model of the world and way of managing things - even if that is almost alien to a neuro-typical individual.

Then, in the conclusion chapter, I round up the topics of loss, dying and death, and break down the triad of impairments (the three areas autistic traits fall into for diagnosis). I go through some areas of these which are common among many with autism, sharing some ideas of what you can do to help the person with autism manage loss, dying and death, as well as some of the additional needs they may have and how these can impact on their handling of loss, dying and death.

CHAPTER TWO

Loss

Loss comes into the topics of death and dying, but I wanted to break these topics down and cover loss separately, because although loss occurs when someone dies, it also occurs in many other areas of life. From relationships ending, through to changing circumstances, like moving from one school to another, or one workplace to another, or moving out of home to live independently.

We all experience loss throughout our lives, from the moment we become aware of others. Toddlers are dependent on their caregivers, and experience loss if the caregiver isn't present when they need something. As they grow up, they usually develop theory of mind where they become aware that when the caregiver isn't around. The caregiver hasn't disappeared; he/she is still thinking about them and still there if you scream loudly to get their attention.

Some children can be anxious, others calm and relaxed about things. This difference is a mix of nature and nurture. If the caregiver is anxious, then they will be teaching the child to respond to things in an anxious way. If the mother was highly anxious - or anxious for a prolonged period during the last trimester before birth - then the child can be born as if the world is full of threats. They can have a lower threshold to stress, leading to them getting anxious quicker than other children.

If the child has a predisposition to being anxious, then when the parent leaves the room, the child will be likely to feel at increased risk and less safe. If they are generally calm and relaxed about things, then they are likely to be calmer when the parent leaves the room. If they are developing normally, then regardless of whether they are more anxious or calm in general, they will be apprehensive when the parent leaves the room. If they are left alone with a stranger, then the anxious child may start crying, whereas the calmer child may just be quieter and not so playful while they wait for their parent to return.

For those with autism, they are likely to take much longer than neurotypical children to develop this awareness that a parent leaving a room doesn't mean they are gone for good. Often, though, children with autism will be unfazed; they don't usually form the same types of attachments that other children form, so being in a room with a stranger is no different to being in a room with their parent. What might make them react with anger or anxiety is a change of routine. They are unlikely to be comfortable with their routine changing, so if they perceive the parent being in the room as being part of the routine, then they may become agitated and angry or anxious (if the parent leaves to answer the phone mid-play, for example).

As they grow up and start thinking about things more, this can increase in frequency, because they will be more likely to make judgements about what they think the plan of action is, rather than being more passive and less analytical when they were younger. So, if they thought that they were going somewhere and were going to 'play with mum' and then mum leaves the room, this changes the routine. This behaviour isn't about loss as such, although loss has happened, but about the shifting routine that is causing that reaction.

When I was a toddler and I was taken to my first day of nursery school, my mum took me to the school and sent me in. I walked in without looking back, without acknowledging her. I didn't experience loss at being separated from my mum. At the time, mum thought this was because I must have such a good attachment to her and good theory of mind that I knew she would be there at the end of the day - that I wasn't losing her and that she was still thinking about me while I'm in nursery school. Mum described how proud she was of this, because most of the other children were crying and were uncomfortable with leaving their parents.

I have three younger brothers, so as the years went by, mum had the opportunity to see how they all reacted in similar situations. They reacted by getting upset and not wanting to leave mum to go into school on their first day. As a toddler, naturally I didn't analyse my thinking about loss, but it was certainly very different to most others my age. I didn't have the same kind of deep attachment to my mum that others had to theirs. I appeared grown-up because of this. To me, a parent leaving me alone in a room was meaningless, because I was in my own world and not interested in who was or wasn't around me.

I think having my kind of outlook around loss protected me from sadness. Since adulthood, loss has caused sadness. Having autism doesn't mean not having emotions, but my reaction is different to others, so the sadness is limited.

When I was a teenager I used to wonder whether I was a psychopath, due in part to how little I cared about other people. I didn't hate people, I was just indifferent – obviously the fact that I had these thoughts was a sign I wasn't a psychopath! As an adult, I have worked extensively with parents of children with autism spectrum disorder, and many have described their concerns about their child not appearing to care - how they are cold and don't consider others.

When children form friendships in school with other children and then they change school, they can experience loss of friends. Most children miss their friends, but loss usually first starts having a noticeable impact on children when they start dating.

I remember dating in secondary school. I had very little interest in others. I was happy to sit on my own, climb trees, and read books on magic or science. It wasn't that I didn't find girls attractive, I just didn't think about trying to go out with any of them until one day when I had been asking a girl out for one of my friends. She came across as a kind and friendly person. For some reason, my friend wanted to date her but didn't want to ask her out himself so they asked me to ask her out for him. After asking her out and her telling me 'no', I decided that actually I would quite like to go out with her. I've no idea why I thought that, or what was different about this moment in time than before, but I had made the decision that I wanted to ask her out. It was around Valentine's Day, so I made her an anonymous card which I slipped into her bag one lunch time. I drew my name in the card in the form of pictures that I drew as a clue to my identity. I didn't think about what she would think of this, I just knew that Valentine's Day was a time to anonymously share a card with the person you would like to be dating.

A few days later, I thought about how I would ask this girl out. I had asked her out for other people and then fed back to them that she had said 'no', but I don't like uncertainty, so I needed to think about how I would respond to her decision. In reality, she was either going to say 'yes' or 'no', so I needed to work out what I could do in both of these situations. When asking her out for other people, I would have a clear course of action; whether she said 'yes' or 'no', I would say 'okay' and then go back to my friend to tell them the answer. The difficulty was that, as the recipient of the message, I couldn't say 'okay' and then dash off to feed that back to anyone… Just dashing off wouldn't be for a legitimate reason!

In the end, I decided to wait until a couple of minutes before the school bell went for the end of lunch time, knowing that if she said 'no', the bell would ring and I would be able to say 'okay' and have a reason for leaving straightaway. As it turned out, she said 'yes'; the bell rang and we didn't have time to talk, so we agreed to meet later and I dashed off to registration.

On the first evening we spent time together, we went back to her home. On entering, I saw the Valentine's Day card I had made for her on the fireplace in the living room. I mentioned that I had made the card. It turned out she had suspected that but didn't know for sure. I showed her how I had hidden my name throughout the pictures I had drawn. This was my first girlfriend. We seemed to get on well, and she came across as kind and caring. I tried to behave how I thought a boyfriend should behave. I was polite and tried to copy the positive behaviours boyfriends exhibited on television programmes and films.

But one flaw that I had was that I didn't think about her and her thoughts. I could replicate what I saw on television programmes and films, but it didn't cross my mind to think about other people's thoughts and perspectives. So, if I was doing something else, I wouldn't pay any attention or give any thought to her. It wouldn't cross my mind that she could be annoyed with me not spending time with them. In my mind, I didn't want to spend time with them at that moment, so why would it be an issue?

I suspect this contributed to my first relationship ending. One evening when I was at a youth club with the girl I was dating, I was doing my own thing, playing pool and not spending time with her, when a boy from my year came up to me. He grabbed me by my collar, pinned me to a wall, started shouting and swearing at me as he told me that he was now going out with that girl, and that I was not to see her ever again. I don't remember feeling particularly intimidated, I didn't retaliate or try to stop him from assaulting me – it didn't cross my mind to do this. I remember thinking that he could have just told me - I didn't understand the need for aggression. I just accepted what I was told as being fact. I never went and spoke with the girl to find out what her real opinion was, or to find out whether the boy's assertion was true, or what her reason was for not wanting to be with me. It didn't cross my mind. I just told the other teen 'okay' and I carried on as if nothing had happened. I never saw the girl again.

I had experienced people dying before this, which I will talk about in the chapter on death, but this was probably my first experience of loss not associated with the death of someone, and my reaction to it was like nothing had happened. Looking back now, I can see how this behaviour could appear cold and uncaring. I didn't get upset and I didn't try to fight to be with the girl I wanted to be with. I just accepted everything and continued on with my life. Others at the time may have thought, perhaps, that I didn't really want to be with her if I was able to walk away that easily.

The reality is, the way that I process things mentally is black and white. So, once I was told I was no longer going out with the girl, I accepted this and my reality was instantly one in which I was not in a relationship with that person. I didn't have feelings of loss; I didn't think about how I had lost something from my life, because my perception of life isn't about gains and losses, it's about 'this is what life is right now'. I struggle to get out of the moment and connect to the bigger picture, and I struggle even more to connect emotionally to things. Whilst with the girl, I would say that I loved her unconditionally, but once the relationship was over, I accepted this and moved on. I find it difficult to explain or justify my innate thinking about things, and people do challenge me about how I can't really have loved them because of how quickly I was able to move on, but this is how I think. I find it frustrating when I am told that I am wrong about my own thinking - that either I'm bottling things up, or that I never really liked someone as much as I thought I did.

This girl was the only girl in school whom I wanted to date to the extent I asked her out. I dated many other girls in school, often lasting somewhere from a day or two up to a couple of months, but these were all girls who asked me out; if I felt they seemed like they were kind and friendly, and if I found them attractive, then I would say 'yes' to them.

In all cases, they were the ones who ended up leaving me. I never asked them why they left me, it didn't cross my mind to be interested in this. I would just say 'okay' and accept it. With some of the girls, I can think of reasons why they probably left me - mainly, probably, my lack of interest in them. I would be very neglectful in the relationships. I would always put myself first unless I was supposed to be with them.

So if I had planned not to be with them one evening and they turned up, I would carry on with the evening I had planned and would totally ignore them; if they then asked why I was ignoring them, I would tell them I was getting on with what I'd planned to do that evening. I didn't see it as ignoring them, because there was no intent to ignore them. I was just paying attention to doing other things. Likewise, if we hadn't made plans, I wouldn't think of spending time with them or making plans with them. They had to put all of the work into the relationship. Unlike the first girl I went out with, all of these other girls told me themselves that they didn't want to go out with me anymore.

I never experienced any feelings from the loss of any of these girlfriends. In every case, they left me. I didn't decide to end any of the relationships. I never had any bad feelings towards any of these girls, and it wasn't that I somehow think in an arrogant way about being better than them, or too good for them - the kind of thing people have said to me based on my indifferent reaction. With every girl I went out with, I was fine being in a relationship with them; I wasn't wishing I wasn't in the relationship, because if I didn't want it, I would have told them that directly. However, the way my mind works, I moved on. In all these teen relationships, there wasn't any point when I had an emotional reaction to the breakup.

In a professional capacity, I have worked with others with autism who have been very upset by the end of relationships, so not all those with autism react the same, but I think there are similarities in how most react. Some whom I have seen react emotionally still seem to think in black and white, and they see it as all or nothing. When the relationship has ended, they react like it is the end of the world, as if that was the love of their life, or the only person they could ever love. They wonder what is left for them: how could they ever find love again? Some have even developed an obsession for the person they were in a relationship with. Sometimes, it is this obsession which has contributed to the person ending the relationship; but the other person still has the obsession and can find it difficult to let go.

If someone has been spending most of the time during the relationship saying they love you and then they leave you, then the natural assumption is that they lied about loving you. If they did love you, they wouldn't have left you. I know for myself that someone lying can be difficult to handle - I can get very angry about it - but at the same time, I seem to be able to think in a logical way that helps me to recognise some lies as being the logical behaviour for the person. I struggle when I can't think of a logical reason for the lying and I personally would struggle to lie like others do, even though I can understand why they have done it.

For parents with children who respond to loss as if they didn't care about what they lost, their response doesn't necessarily mean they didn't care; they probably just responded by compartmentalising things. So, if a child or teen was in a relationship, they probably cared about the other person while they were in the relationship. Once the relationship ended, if they suddenly moved on, this may just mean they have accepted that the relationship had ended.

It isn't helpful to push these children to 'have feelings' or to criticise them for not being upset and for not caring – either about the person, or about the loss of the person. This is an assumption being made based on how the person making the assumption thinks and feels about things, so it is a reflection on them. It doesn't mean that the child should also think or feel the same. It can be useful to sit with the child to explore what happened and what their thoughts are about it; that being said, you are unlikely to get feeling statements from them. So they may say they liked being with the person, but they are okay with the relationship being over, because it is what the other person wanted. Or if it was moving schools, for example, and they no longer see certain friends they seemed to be close to, they may say they liked them but it doesn't occur to them to make contact with their friend.

When I left primary school to go to secondary school, it didn't cross my mind to keep in touch with any friends, and I didn't miss any of them. In fact, I don't recall thinking about them at all until I joined Facebook and realised you could connect with people from your past,

An Autistic Perspective: Death, Dying and Loss

and I had curiosity about where they might be now, and what lives different people might have. This wasn't confined to friends, but to everyone I knew. The same happened with secondary school. When I left secondary school, I had telephone numbers and addresses of certain friends, but it never crossed my mind to contact them. I have never thought about meeting up with them to the extent of actually deciding to take action. Since being on Facebook I have wondered what different people are up to. I always want the best for everyone, so I hope that everyone I knew in primary school and secondary school, and from other areas of my life, has gone on to lead the best life possible, but I rarely think about meeting up with people. This is one issue I have that I think is behind numerous lost friendships. I don't often think about meeting up with family, or people I know, so as time passes, so do friends and family.

It doesn't mean I don't like any of these people, just that when someone is out of sight, they are out of mind - unless I see something related to them. If I have a friend interested in Star Trek and I see a reference to Star Trek, I will think about that friend, but that often isn't enough to make me think about contacting them to maintain the relationship. Normally, I only think about contacting someone if I want something, although this has started to change.

Like most people on the autistic spectrum, as I have grown up and my life experience and knowledge have increased, I have developed and changed as a person; certain traits which used to be more extreme have become less extreme. I now have greater insight into my thinking and feelings. I now make some effort from time to time to contact friends and family. I do this not because I suddenly have interest where I previously didn't, but because I know it is what I am supposed to do, so from time to time, I remember I am supposed to contact friends or family and meet with them to see how things are going for them. I listen to them tell me what they have been up to, and I know that I am supposed to do this even when there aren't any known problems going on in their life that they need help with.

I am aware now that if I don't contact them from time to time, they will be the ones always making all of the effort in the relationship, and as time passes, they will contact me less and less until they stop contacting me at all. From my perspective and given past experience, I doubt I would mind, but I am aware that sometimes it is useful to have friends, and to maintain friendships you have to put in effort. Finding and making friends isn't easy, so it is best to try to keep those you have.

How I reacted to my first serious adult relationship was different to how I reacted to relationships as a teenager. Getting in to the relationship was no different. I was direct to the woman about how I found her attractive, and direct about how I wanted to date her. We were in the relationship for some years until one day she told me she no longer wanted to be in a relationship with me. When she told me this, I accepted it just as I had done before when people had told me they didn't want to be in a relationship with me. I agreed to move out of the flat we shared.

A few months earlier, I had suspected she was in a relationship with someone else. I had asked her directly whether she was, and she denied it. When she told me she no longer wanted to be in a relationship with me, suddenly many people who knew us both said that they'd thought she was cheating on me, but none of them had told me this while the two of us were together. I felt that they all kept it a secret for the same reason that she did - they didn't want to hurt my feelings. I don't see that my feelings would have been hurt, but I can understand that they felt this way, and so they felt lying was a better option than telling the truth. When the situation is reversed, this is something I struggle with doing. If I know someone is cheating on their partner, I would just tell the person that they are being cheated on. I am not interested enough to go out of my way to do this, but if I was asked directly, I would give a direct and honest answer.

Despite being in a long-term relationship, sharing many experiences together (both positive and negative), and being married to the person (as a side note, I firmly believe that when you marry you are making a commitment that you will be together until death), and discovering that she was cheating on me, when she told me, I accepted this and just walked away. There were only three times I showed emotion in relation to this relationship ending.

The first was the last time I walked away from the flat with my last box of belongings. My best friend and I went to the flat to pick up the last of my things to take back to my new place. As we left, my wife showed us out and he went off ahead. I stopped briefly to say goodbye so I ended up a dozen or so paces behind him. After walking a little way, I've no idea why, but I stopped to look back. I think I had the thought that this was the last time I was going to be here and this made me take one last look. By this time, my best friend had stopped walking and turned to face me. As I turned and looked back at the front door, I could see my wife stood in the doorway crying. Suddenly I felt aching around my sinuses and tears coming to my eyes. I turned from the flat and carried on walking towards my best friend. Almost as soon as I had turned away from the flat the tears in my eyes cleared up and I felt the same as I had when I was last looking in this direction.

The second time I expressed emotion was a few weeks later. My then-partner and I were struggling for money. I had a computer. She asked if we could sell the computer and split the money. She said she knew someone who wanted to buy it and pointed out that we both needed the money. I agreed that sounded fine and gave her the computer to sell. A week or so later, I hadn't heard anything about the money, so I contacted her and was told: 'If I wanted money, I should sell something else of mine'. This made me instantly see red and get angry. I was angry about being lied to. I wasn't angry about the loss and then this happening; it was more the case that I was lied to without any logical reason. If she had wanted the computer to sell and wanted to keep all the money for herself, she could have just told me this and I would have given her the computer. But to say she was going to split the money and then not to do this - that was lying, and it made no sense to lie. At the time, those around me were telling me that I was overreacting because I hadn't been getting emotional about the relationship ending. They felt that I was bottling up and repressing my feelings, and now they were coming out in anger with the computer situation being a focal point for all of my feelings. It didn't matter how much I keep saying that I wasn't doing this, that I had moved on and accepted my situation just fine, they couldn't relate to this. They could only think about how they felt that they would react.

Being lied to when I can't see a logical reason for it and having plans change are two things I struggle with, even to this day. This is what made me angry and emotional in this situation, I was angry about being lied to, and about the plan changing, rather than the loss. I was angry for just a short while before the anger cleared, and I carried on as if nothing had happened.

The third time I got emotional was on my first wedding anniversary. I hadn't been married long when the relationship ended, and I believe when you get married you are making a commitment to say that you love each other and that you will stay together until death; on the first anniversary, I started thinking about how it would have been my first year. I began questioning whether I had thrown the relationship away. At this point, I was in a happy relationship with the person who would go on to be my current wife, but on that day, I suddenly became aware of thoughts about how I behaved, and insights about whether my behaviour was the correct course of action. I had never thought about my behaviour prior to this. If I walked away from a relationship, it had no impact on me, but for some reason this was different.

On that day, I was on annual leave, I found myself drinking a couple of bottles of Absinthe during the day because I was finding it difficult having thoughts about whether I should have refused to leave. I thought about whether the right decision would have been to fight for my marriage - whether I was too quick to accept what she had said. Because I generally assume that people tell the truth, when she told me she didn't want to be with me, I accepted it as being the only option. To me, if she didn't mean it, then she wouldn't have said it. Perhaps she would have said that she didn't know whether she wanted to be with me, which would have meant that she was undecided. But

An Autistic Perspective: Death, Dying and Loss

she was certain in what she'd said. My thoughts now were around the fact that we had both promised to be together until death, and so there was a conflict. She had promised this too, and part of the promise was to stick together even through difficult times. Yet, the first difficult time since being married, instead of trying to work things out, we separated.

I found it difficult having these thoughts in my mind. I had never contemplated my thinking in this way before. I had never questioned my way of thinking, or whether there was an alternative way. In everything up to this point, I believed everything everyone said as being the truth; if I found out that they had lied it was usually later, not having noticed they were lying at the time. In most cases I could understand their logic for lying. If someone said they didn't want to be with me, I accepted it, moved on, and never thought about it again. If someone told me something was happening – like a change in work – again, I accepted it as something that would happen; if I didn't like it then I would tell my employers this, and if they said they were still going to make the changes whether I liked it or not, then I would leave the job before those changes happened. I wouldn't fight to change people's minds. I would accept their decision as fixed and unchanging. But, all of a sudden, I was questioning whether things people said were definitely the final answer.

By the end of that day, I had accepted that whatever decisions were made had been made, so really it was illogical to be suddenly questioning this. I was in a relationship with someone else now. I wanted to be in this new relationship, and all I was doing by thinking about decisions made in the past, and by drinking, was negatively impacting on the new relationship with the person who has gone on to be my wife, and with whom I've now been in a relationship for about 16 years.

Although I decided it was illogical to think about past decisions like this, it made me aware that I have this black-and-white thinking style where I accept things people say without questioning them. I imagine there is no doubt, just certainty, on behalf of the person talking to me.

I was aware that in the future, in loss situations, I should aim to remember to consider my way of thinking before making my own final decisions and accepting things I'm told. Although I am aware of this, I still find it difficult to do. I am approaching 40 years old. I have a lot of insight into myself, my thoughts, feelings, and behaviours compared to what I had when I was in my early twenties, yet I still respond the same as I did back then. I still walk away from loss by accepting it straightaway and moving on. When I have lost jobs, or been turned down for jobs, I haven't fought my corner; I've accepted what I have been told and walked away. It is only many months later that the thought will cross my mind, that perhaps I could have fought to show I was right for the job. But because I can't change the past, these thoughts are fleeting - just semblances of alternative decisions that I could have tried making.

When my relationship ended, it was only about a month before I saw the woman who is now my wife. As soon as I had the chance, I told her that I wanted to date her. Initially, people felt that I wanted to date her as a rebound thing, because I had just come out of a long-term relationship. Friends were telling me that, following the end of my relationship, I should be angry and sad, and that I should be going out drinking heavily and sleeping around. I was also told that it should take many months for me to move on, and if I moved on sooner, then I was considered to be bottling my feelings up.

I rarely drank by this point in my life. I had been a heavy social drinker in my teens, but stopped drinking for a year when I was 19. Since then I drank very little and very infrequently, but friends would drag me out to the pub with them because they felt it wasn't good for me to be in a flat alone when I had just come out of a relationship. I just went with what they said. I didn't try to 'pull' lots of women like they were saying I should, because this isn't me and I have no interest in doing this, but I did end up meeting my current wife and we started going out with each other. I don't think she ever thought I was only with her as a rebound relationship, though many people I knew thought this. It didn't matter what I said about how I genuinely had moved on from the relationship which had just ended; they wouldn't believe me. I remember finding this frustrating, because I felt that they were disregarding my reality - my views and opinions - as being wrong and there was nothing I could say to convince them otherwise. They would talk about me repressing things and said that it would come out somewhere, sometime.

It wasn't helpful to have my thoughts and feelings disregarded in this way at a time of loss. It would have been more helpful to have acceptance around how I experience and process things, and understanding that this is different to how they worked. Sometimes, people with autism will process their experience of the world differently to others and this should be accepted non-judgementally; it should not be interpreted as the individual not caring, or being cold because they have moved on too quickly, but accepted as just a different way of reacting to things.

Leaving home and moving into your own place is another time of loss. At this time, you separate from family, from the home and environment you know, to a new home with new routines, new responsibilities and new challenges. For those with autism, this can be a difficult time. Generally, those with autism don't like change. With moving out, they have suddenly had a big change, so there is a lot to get used to, as well as managing the loss of what they'd had previously.

When I left home, I didn't think about keeping in touch with my family, and I didn't telephone or write to them. Because they were out of sight, they were out of mind. I never thought about them, or about going and visiting them. It wasn't until I was in a relationship a couple of years later that my girlfriend at the time said I should see them and make effort for them, because they are my family. Prior to this, the only time I saw them was if they happened to be in my work. I worked in a holiday camp, so my mum, step-dad, brothers and grandparents would sometimes make day visits during school holidays. My nan would occasionally write to me, and my parents and grandparents would send me birthday and Christmas cards, but it didn't occur to me to reciprocate this. This didn't mean I disliked them, I just didn't think about them.

So, moving out of home and into my own flat meant that I stopped seeing my family. I imagine that some parents would find this difficult and would perhaps think that maybe their autistic son or daughter doesn't love them, or some other interpretation, when in reality, their son or daughter may just not be giving them any thought at all. It isn't that they don't love their family, their family just isn't in their mind that often when they aren't in sight.

To me, moving out was the loss of a family unit, the loss of a home, the loss of a life without real commitments. It was the loss of childhood and the gaining of a strange new world of adulthood. I quickly turned to heavy drinking as a way of coping with this new world. I was working in a holiday camp, where the expectation was to socialise with others, but I struggled with social interaction; I would drink alcohol because it was the socially acceptable thing to do when you are in a nightclub or bar. Continual drinking was a way of continually looking busy: 'I just finished a drink; I'd better go to the bar and get another one'... 'mouthful of drink so I can't talk'... 'drink in hand so I can't go and dance'... 'looking at my drink so I can't see you trying to get my attention' (and noisy club so I can't hear you!)... 'just finished my drink, got to go because I need the loo', and so on.

When I left home, I quickly ended up drinking in excess of 18 pints of *Snakebite and Black* per night and by the age of 18 had progressed on to about three bottles of *Jack Daniel's* and other spirits like *Pernod, Ouzo, Vodka, Southern Comfort,* or *Absinthe* per night. I often mixed them in a pint glass, gulping down the pint at the beginning of the evening, before continuing drinking through to about 4am, and starting work at 7am. This became my way of fitting in and coping with the new situation following the loss of being part of a family and the loss of my home.

This new routine was obviously not what my family would have wanted for me, but once I had to find a new routine, I latched onto the easiest one that I could. I worked long hours – during the summer months, 7am to 11pm, six days per week. This was the time I formed my new routines. I went straight from work to going drinking with colleagues and then back to work. This was the routine that presented itself; this was the routine that quickly freed me from the uncertainty and fear of doing my new job and meeting all these new people. I managed to end up working in a pot wash where I was able to set my own routine and where I had reduced contact with other work colleagues.

I think if I had been diagnosed with autism spectrum disorder as a child or teen, then I would have had support around the transition between school and work, and the loss of one lifestyle and the beginning of a new one. I perhaps would have had support with family visiting me, because they would understand that it wouldn't cross my mind to make contact with them or anyone else, regardless of how bad things got. There were times I wouldn't have electricity - I wouldn't have heat, or hot water and I didn't have food, but I didn't think to ask for help, I just accepted my situation for what it was.

As I mention throughout this book, not everyone with autism perceives things the same, so others may well find loss difficult to deal with. I believe it is a myth that autistic people lack emotions (something many people have told me), but my personal and professional experiences tell me otherwise. I think those with autism can get sensory overload with emotions, just like any other sense, and I think this is why many people with autism can find that they feel either nothing, or overwhelming emotion, because even the slightest emotion feels overwhelming. I think the difference is that those with autism have emotional reactions at different times to most other people, and in a different way. I think it is usually compartmentalised, so the emotion is closely linked to something specific, and perhaps overwhelming to that specific thing; around that, there may well be no emotion.

So, although when it comes to loss, I respond generally in an unemotional way, others may respond highly emotionally and may need support through the loss. They are likely to need help getting into a new routine and handling uncertainty, as those with autism can become obsessed with things. If they have developed an obsession for a person, for example, and suddenly lose the focus of their obsession, then this can be a huge shock and change to their life with which they need to come to terms. As well as having to develop a new routine and tackle the sudden uncertainty, they will also have to address the obsession, because they may still be obsessed. If it is a person who has broken up with them, then this could be a problem, especially with their all-or-nothing thinking and possibly high levels of emotion.

CHAPTER THREE

Dying & Death

Dying and death is a natural part of living. From the moment we are born, it is inevitable that we will die. As my favourite psychiatrist, Milton H Erickson MD, once said: "Some people just do it more efficiently than others."

I have always been fascinated with death and dying. I think this is partly because of the certainty. Since learning about science, and learning that death is a process, and a process that happens differently across all life, with some animals living longer than others (and some plants and trees living for hundreds or thousands of years, and some animals like the *Turritopsis dohrnii* jellyfish being immortal if they can avoid predators, disease and accidental death), I have always wanted every being to have the best life possible and as little suffering as possible. That said, I am aware I can sound uncaring at times when I talk about death and dying. I have never thought about how I talk as being uncaring, but I have had people tell me this on many occasions, so I know it is something people think at times.

I have always been comfortable talking about death and dying, and confused about why others aren't comfortable talking about these topics, given that they, too, are inevitable aspects of life. We all go through a period of dying; we will all die, we will all know others who are dying, and we will experience the death of others. It seems logical to me that from a young age, we should be comfortable talking about death and dying, and addressing how we can think and behave around these topics.

When I was growing up, I remember my nan telling me that children should have pets, because the pets will die and this helps children to learn about death. It helps them to understand for when people die in their life as they grow up. I grew up with pets. I am not a religious person, but I grew up in my earliest years with my parents being Jehovah's Witnesses. This was mainly my dad's influence - it was he and his side of the family who were Jehovah's Witnesses, and so mum became one. After my mum and dad separated and my mum remarried, she stopped being a Jehovah's Witness but still had my brothers and myself attending church every Sunday. I also attended a catholic primary school where we sang hymns and prayed and went to the local Cathedral during the week.

As a primary school child, I didn't think anything of it; I assumed this was what people did. I assumed God was real, because everyone around me talked about God as if they were talking about something real. I didn't think to question or doubt what I was told. The local youth group I attended as a primary school child was a religious group where they gave us leaflets with comics about tales from the bible and information about Christianity and how we should be living life. All of this was given as if it was fact. It was all given so sincerely that I didn't think to question any of it.

I remember when my goldfish died. I took it outside in a little pot, dug a small hole and buried it and placed a cross made out of ice-cream sticks to mark where it was buried. I assumed this is what you were supposed to do when a death occurs. I didn't feel upset - it was a goldfish, and things die. I was curious about what it would look like weeks later and so went back and dug it up to take a look. I didn't know why I was supposed to bury the goldfish. As a child, other pets of mine, or of my brothers, died. By the time I was about 8 years old, I had begun learning about science, and by the time I started secondary school I didn't believe there was a God. I couldn't find any evidence for one, or a need for one. That said, in relation to death and dying, I could understand that those who believed in God seemed to find comfort from their beliefs when people in their lives died. I also liked that religions taught about love, kindness, respect and tolerance for others.

Once I stopped believing in God I also couldn't understand the rituals around death. They seemed to bring people comfort; they would bring people together, and those people would unite in grief and sadness at the loss of their loved one. The ritual seemed to be more for the benefit of friends and relatives of the person who died, rather than serving any purpose for the deceased. When I was younger, I used to think that these rituals were somehow to do with helping the person move on to a spiritual place, like heaven, but now I felt it was actually for the friends and family.

In primary school, I had experienced the death of the headmistress, and soon after that, the death of her husband who also taught at the school from time to time. Just after I left the primary school, a friend of mine died too. I didn't find any of these deaths upsetting, and they all came without warning, so while I had experienced death, I hadn't experienced the process of others around me dying at that point.

My first experience with someone dying was an uncle of mine. He was a very kind man, but a heavy smoker. By the time he thought about quitting smoking, he had terminal lung cancer. He looked in pain and was clearly suffering and aware that he was going to die. This motivated him to stop smoking, but by that time it was too late to save his life. This was the first time I had known someone who was dying. His wife, my aunty, appeared to find it upsetting, but I didn't feel anything about it. I felt that he had decided to smoke, and part of deciding to do something which may kill you is accepting that you may die from it. I was only a teenager at this time - I didn't have anything to do with the care of my uncle, and I only saw him once following his lung cancer diagnosis.

Dan Jones

I think as a child and teenager I probably experienced death and dying like most children do. They don't fully understand what is going on, or they don't connect emotionally with what is going on. I know some children and teens do find death upsetting, but from the work I have done with families, it seems that children are pretty resilient and, as long as they have positive support and guidance from their parents, they handle things well. They miss the dead loved one, but they don't get too upset about it. I think this starts to change as children grow up and they become teenagers, because they start to understand death differently; they comprehend it as something that is permanent, and they understand that they will never see that person again.

I was aware that I wouldn't see people who had died again, but that didn't really upset me. Even now, when I am much older, I don't really feel upset about not seeing someone again; for me, it is more about the memories and not wanting who they were to be lost.

In 2000, I had an uncle whom I looked up to die. This uncle used to be a magician. He used to also be in plays. He was funny, and he was creative and inventive. For my eleventh birthday my uncle had bought me a science book which was clearly aimed at an older audience. My mum wanted to return the book to him, stating that it was too advanced for a child of my age. I told her I wanted to keep it. I read that book over and over again. This wasn't the first present he had bought me that wasn't necessarily appropriate for children. A couple of years earlier, he had given me a magic tricks book which taught how to do sword-swallowing and fire-eating, amongst other things!

My uncle was also a keen photographer. I used to visit him in his bungalow near the seafront. We would walk along the seafront with his SLR camera. He taught me about composition and how to take different types of photographs, then we would go back to his bungalow and develop the photos in his bathroom. He even taught me how to turn the matt-finish black-and-white photographs into glossy prints by wetting them, then sticking them on the window.

An Autistic Perspective: Death, Dying and Loss

I used to find him so knowledgeable and interesting, and would take every opportunity I could to spend time with him, learning from him. Even after I left home, he would send me cards with riddles or puzzles on them, then I would respond with what I thought the answer was, and would send him riddles and puzzles in return.

For most of my childhood, I remember obsessing about wanting to know what was in his 'magic' suitcases. Sometimes, my brothers and I would be sleeping at my grandparents. He would turn up having given a magic show somewhere and he would have these two big locked suitcases with him. I remember saying frequently as a child that when he died, I hoped to inherit his magic suitcases. I used to practice magic tricks all the time and looked forward to when I would be at my grandparents' house when he would be there so that I could put on a magic show for him, to show what I had learned since I last saw him. He was about the only person I related to as a child, because I found everything about him interesting. I wanted to learn everything he seemed to have to teach.

In 2000, my uncle heard the lifeboat maroons sound, so, as he had done dozens of times before, he rushed to the mouth of the River Arun in Littlehampton to take photographs of the lifeboats going out to sea and returning into the river again. He took some photographs as they went out, and then there was an incident down the river, so as they came back in, they did so much faster than usual. At the river mouth, where the sea water comes in meeting the fresh water going out, there is an area of rough water. He had always wanted to get a photograph of the lifeboat with lots of spray, but the boat was usually too slow as it entered, so the photographs were always lacking this, but with the lifeboat heading to an emergency in the river it was travelling faster. As it hit the swollen water and jumped on the waves, spray came up around it and he managed to take the picture he had spent years trying to capture.

This was the last photo on the film in the camera, which was in his hand when he was found dead by a walker on the beach. A blood clot had gotten to his heart and killed him so quickly he didn't have time to drop his camera or clutch his chest. It appeared he'd died instantly, and the last thing he probably saw was that image of the lifeboat he had just taken.

When I got the telephone call to say my uncle had died I was at home. My mum gave the news in a matter-of-fact way. I took the news in a matter-of-fact way. The only time I cried was as I was telling my girlfriend just after receiving this news. She found it upsetting, and although I didn't physically feel anything, and didn't think I was upset by the news, I cried at seeing her cry.

A couple of weeks later, I received a letter from my nan sharing the story above and containing the photographs my uncle had taken of the lifeboat on that day.

What I found interesting was that my uncle's death seemed to upset my girlfriend more than it upset me. She was upset about his death, and also upset *for me*. I couldn't understand why she found it so hard. She had only met him once or twice. She had heard me talking about him a number of times, but didn't really know him. I also couldn't understand why she was upset for me. This seemed strange. I can understand people being upset because something upsetting has happened to them, but why should they be upset when something upsetting has happened to someone else?

Because she knew I obviously liked my uncle, she felt I was bottling my feelings up, because my attitude was that it was a shame he had died, but that he had died. There was nothing that could change this. Getting sad didn't change that fact, being sad didn't change my memories, and his death didn't take away my memories either. So although there would be no new memories formed with him, I could still think about old memories whenever I wanted. I wasn't bottling anything up, I just couldn't see the logic in being upset. Apart from crying when I was passing the news on to my girlfriend, I have never been too sad about his death – I also ended up inheriting his 'magic' suitcases.

An Autistic Perspective: Death, Dying and Loss

To others, my non-emotional way of handling things can seem cold and uncaring, but it is just that I think about things differently. When someone dies, I don't find the fact that they have died sad; telling someone close to me that someone has died, and seeing them cry, makes me cry. It doesn't matter how much I try to fight this, it happens. I find this strange. Because although my eyes are watering and I am clearly crying, I don't *feel* anything; it is just like my eyes have started watering for some reason. Once I look away from the person who is crying, or I think about something different, my eyes stop watering and I am fine. I wouldn't be able to vocalise an emotion that I am experiencing at this time, I feel neutral. I have thought long and hard about this as I have tried to understand my experiences, and my best guess is that I struggle to be in touch with my emotions – it's almost like there is a mind-body division or disassociation, where my body can experience something without my mind knowing what my body is experiencing.

The next death in my life following the death of my uncle was a girlfriend of mine having a miscarriage. I've always been in two minds about having children. On the one hand, I would like children who can inherit my things when I die and with whom I can share stories to keep the family history alive into future generations. On the other hand, I can't imagine myself being any good as a parent. I've spent most of my adult life working with children and families. I had thousands of hours of training around the topics of parenting, child development and family support work. I have worked with thousands of families and helped with a wide range of issues, from violence in children and teens, to helping implement effective parenting strategies. I've worked in residential children's homes with children and teens, and so much more. Yet I still think I wouldn't be capable of being a good parent. I'm aware that this is how many people think, so I am generally ambivalent to this; I think that I would have to just go with the flow.

When I was 22, my girlfriend became pregnant. After a couple of months, we told friends and family. I started to think about the idea of having a baby at 23. I thought about how this would actually be quite a good age to be a father, because when the child was 16 I would still have been under 40, and hopefully fit and healthy enough to be running around with them. I thought about how being young parents would mean our child would hopefully have parents for many years to come, and if they had children, they would have grandparents for many years. I thought about what it would be like to have children at 40 or 50, and how I would have been 56 or 66 when they were 16, and perhaps 66 to 76 by the time they had children of their own.

I was comfortable with the idea of being a father at 23, despite not feeling that our life situation was ideal for having a baby around the flat. We had already got a date set to get married, so we would also have been married by the time the baby was due. Then, one day, my girlfriend had been to the toilet. She felt like something was wrong, and while on the toilet she noticed a tiny spot of blood. This was enough for us to visit the hospital.

The hospital did a scan and told us that the baby was dead. My girlfriend started to cry. I found that her crying bought tears to my eyes. A doctor came and spoke with us and told us that this was our fault that the baby was dead, because we were too young to be parents – she was 20, and I 22. He then told us we could either go home and at some point the baby would come out of my girlfriend, or they could remove the baby there and then in the hospital. My girlfriend decided that she would rather have the baby removed, than have a traumatic experience of it coming out at some random future time.

Despite going on to get married at a rearranged date almost a year later, this event was the beginning of the end of our relationship. At 22 years old, I had read some books on hypnosis, and had worked for a few years in homes for people with mental health challenges, and had even just started working in a residential children's home, but I didn't have the knowledge, skills or understanding that I have now about interpersonal communication skills. I could match someone's behaviour, and use this to build rapport. I could do fake smiles that looked quite convincing, and I could use vague language and vague responses to cover up that I had no idea what people were going on about. But, I couldn't really empathise; I didn't understand how people thought differently to me, although I knew in certain situations they definitely appeared to do so. Nor did it cross my mind to appear to care or be supportive.

I have always been told that I am a kind and friendly person by those who know me. I would give a hug if I was hugged, but I definitely wasn't observant enough about the behaviours of others, let alone interpreting behaviours. So, when my girlfriend lost the baby, she was upset and we hugged on the way home. If she came to me for a hug we would hug, but I didn't think to instigate this. We both had very different thinking going on.

The situation was sad. A baby had died before it was even born. It hadn't had the chance to lead a life yet. I processed this logically; I knew it was sad and then moved on. I am aware that although this attitude sounds flippant, this was genuinely my experience. I am also, paradoxically, aware that it must have had an impact on me because even today writing this 17 years later, I can remember the due date of the baby – 21st October. I don't remember the exact date that we went to the hospital, I don't remember the original date we had planned to get married, but I do remember the date I expected to be a dad.

I went back to work on my next shift as if nothing had happened. I told a work colleague of mine in a matter-of-fact way because we worked 24-hour shifts together, so in my opinion, it was important for her to know, due to the nature of the work. The teens would somehow manage to find emotional weaknesses in staff and play on those weaknesses until the staff snapped in anger. I didn't think this would be something that they could somehow pick up on and use, but I was aware that there is always that chance, and so the safest thing to do is tell your colleagues so that they were appraised. Fortunately, nothing ever happened.

My girlfriend remained upset by the experience and became increasingly depressed over time. I didn't really pick up on this. I never spoke with her about the miscarriage, or asked her about it, because it never crossed my mind to do so. A year or so after we separated, she told me that she never spoke to me about it because she was worried I was probably already hurting as much as she was, and she didn't want to upset me further. On reflection, this lack of communication, and lack of me noticing what was going on for my girlfriend, was at the heart of us breaking up. I carried on like normal, as if nothing had happened from the day we had been in hospital, whereas my girlfriend was going over the experience in her mind. She was blaming herself, most likely encouraged by the comments of the doctor; she felt everything was her fault, and that all she did was bring pain and upset to people. I didn't pick up on any of this.

I didn't receive my diagnosis of autism spectrum disorder until many years later, but I feel that this situation may have gone better had I been diagnosed as a child or teenager. My girlfriend may have then known that I thought in a specific way, and that I wouldn't pick up on how she was feeling, and so she would need to tell me. Likewise, I would have known that I thought differently, and we would have been able to have discussions about this. This is where I am at in my current relationship. My wife knows what I am like, and I know that we think differently. I need her to be blunt, open and honest with me so that I know what is going in her mind and what role she would like me to play, and I am aware she is unlikely to handle situations the same way that I do. I have to ask her questions about how she is feeling and thinking about things, and make an effort to show interest, and to be supportive, even when it wouldn't ordinarily cross my mind. I can easily sit in a room on my own and not interact with anyone; I won't think about what the other person may think or feel about something, because my natural assumption is that they think and feel how they are deciding to think and feel. My wife regularly tells me that most people don't decide how they will think and feel; it happens automatically, and they don't feel they have much control over it.

An Autistic Perspective: Death, Dying and Loss

Although everyone with autism spectrum disorder will respond differently in this kind of situation, there are likely to be some similarities. Most will probably process the emotions differently to their partner. They may feel upset but not know how to show it, or may feel overwhelmed with emotion. Many are likely to appear colder and less caring, because they may unknowingly compartmentalise their emotional response, so thinking about the baby may make them very upset, but thinking about something else may quickly put them in a different frame of mind. They may struggle to grasp their partner's experience, and not realise that their partner is perhaps deeply upset and may even be struggling internally with what they are going through.

The best advice I would give is common sense: communicate, and be honest with each other. Ask each other how you can help, so that you can do what the other person says they need to be able to help them through this situation.

In 2014, my wife and I planned on getting married. We decided that we would get married on a Friday 13th, on our 13th anniversary of being together. A few months before the wedding I invited my dad along. A mutual friend had told me that dad had been ill but that he didn't want to tell my brother or me because he didn't want us to be upset. As the wedding approached, my dad's health deteriorated. I still hadn't been to visit him, because he didn't want to upset us with his ill health. I didn't know what was wrong with him, and it didn't cross my mind to ask. He had told our mutual friend that he didn't want us to know he was ill; in short, I knew he was ill because our mutual friend had told me he was ill, but he felt it would be best coming from my dad to say what was wrong.

Nearer to the wedding day, I spoke to dad and told him I was going to visit him. He was talking about possibly not making it to the wedding due to his health, so I felt I should see him and find out what was wrong, to see what could be done to make sure he was able to attend.

Dad argued about how he didn't want me visiting, but I told him that I was doing it, He agreed it would be nice to see me. I went and visited him and he told me that he had oesophageal cancer. He was told it was incurable, but with treatment they may be able to slow his decline down. He was accepting some bits of treatment, but refusing others. He told me he didn't want to upset me or my brother by having us see him look the way he does. He did now look like a very old man, despite only being in his early 60s.

I had done everything I could to make sure that my dad could be at my wedding, but a few days beforehand, he told me he was too ill to attend. After I was married dad's health was rapidly declining. He wasn't well enough to walk further than from one room to another in his flat, and he could only do that by leaning on to things as he walked, and strategically placing chairs along his route from room to room, so that he could sit if he got tired. He was barely eating any food, and was starting to need support. Two good friends of his were visiting and helping him, and my brother had also started going. He still needed more support so I started helping as well.

After a couple of weeks, I took the wedding video to my dad to show him. He sat through the video, largely in silence, with just a few words punctured throughout about how beautiful my wife looked in her wedding dress, how happy we both looked together, and how proud he was of me and all that I have achieved. Dad cried as he watched the video.

As dad's health deteriorated I was visiting him a few times per week, with my brother and two of his friends also supporting him. I was also working full-time, managing, supervising and doing clinical supervisions with a team of family support workers, and running a course for parents and teens to address teen to parent domestic abuse, as well as running a hypnotherapy diploma. As I don't drive, I was also travelling for hours each day to visit my dad. People around me were telling me I was doing too much. Emotionally, I didn't feel like I was doing too much, which is what most people were referring to when the spoke to me about 'doing too much'. I did feel I was overdoing it with how many hours I was putting in per day of being very active, because I would set off for work at 7am and get home at about 11pm, often having not eaten since my lunch break, and many nights dad would telephone me through the night. This was a tiring routine to have, but it wasn't an emotional routine.

As dad was dying, he was often quite difficult. He would demand things to be done his way. If a cup of coffee was made wrong, he would demand that it be taken back to the kitchen, poured away and remade. If a meal was made wrong he would demand that was remade too. My view was that he gets what he is given. He is either hungry or thirsty, or he isn't, and if he is then he will eat or drink what he is given. I think of food and drink as serving a practical purpose; they are there to give energy. I didn't have time when I visited to be remaking food and drink.

Others struggled with dad's stubbornness and bluntness, and his attitude of things having to be done in an exact way. For example, his coffee had to have exactly the correct amount of coffee, one white sugar, one golden sugar, exactly the right amount of milk, and be exactly the right temperature and in the correct cup. Obviously, I would try to make it exactly as he liked it, but if I tried my best and he didn't like it that was tough, I had made it. I wasn't going to make it again.

I didn't mind dad's stubbornness, because I was just blunt with him about how things were going to be if I was doing them. I was willing to accept he didn't want my support if he ever decided that, but if he did want my support, he got it on my terms. I wasn't going to waste my time re-doing food and drinks. Although I was blunt with dad, I was never angry or aggressive or frustrated. I was always calm and relaxed, but assertive. I was aware while supporting my dad that this was how I could so easily turn out. I imagined that if I was single, I wouldn't make any effort to contact anyone, friends or family, and as the years went by I could imagine people stopping making the effort with me. I could become more isolated over time, until I could be this person who reached the end of his life and needed help but didn't ask for it.

My dad dying and suffering was different to when my uncle died of lung cancer caused by smoking when I was a teenager. Dad was also dying due to his smoking, but this time I was far more involved in his life than I had been in my uncle's. I had been to his hospital appointments with him, I had advocated for him, and I had sat with him when he was in pain.

I would be sat in his room while he would be writhing in pain on his bed. He would arch over and contort in agony, he would scream and groan, his eyes would roll back in his head or be wide with a look of terror. His mouth would often be wide open and tense, almost as if his jaw was locked open. He would be like this for hours and his pain and suffering continued most of the day and night every day. When I wasn't there he would telephone dozens of times during the night leaving messages of him screaming in pain and begging for help, and begging to be saved. When I was there, I would sit on the chair near his bed, calmly not saying or doing anything, because I hadn't been told what to say or do. I need guidance and instructions. I need to be told specific tasks and told how to do those tasks. If I don't have that I wait until I do.

Dad wanted me to have initiative and *just know* what to do. He said my brother *just knows* what to do and does it, his friends *just know* what to do and just do it, but I don't. I just sit there. I don't say or do anything to comfort him, I don't decide to go and make him dinner, or a coffee, or to tidy up. I would wait until he told me to do something. He found this frustrating and said I was useless as a carer because all I do is sit there. This was one of the downsides of having autism spectrum disorder; in my head I knew I wanted to be the son my dad wanted me to be. I wanted to be able to use my initiative. I wanted to be proactive, but it just never happened. I couldn't seem to bring myself to behave this way, and I wouldn't think about behaving this way until some time after visits. I didn't feel I had anything to offer Dad other than carrying out practical tasks as asked.

A positive was that I was able to offer care to my dad just like I was a professional care worker. I wasn't emotionally impacted on by his situation or the fact that he was my dad. I didn't feel anything when I sat for hours watching him in agony. But, like when I worked as a care worker almost 20 years earlier, I needed a clear job description and defined jobs with which I was supported to carry out. Any deviation from this, or having to think using my own initiative and I wouldn't know what to do, I would just be in limbo awaiting instructions.

When he briefly spoke about thinking of wanting to end his life to escape all the pain, but needing help to do this if he did, I was clear that I had no problem helping if he ever decided that, because it sounded like the logical decision. He was terminally ill, and his life consisted of minimal sleep, always feeling hungry and struggling to eat, and always in excruciating pain every waking hour of every day throughout his whole body. It definitely seemed logical to me, that if he wanted me to help him take his own life so that he could suffer just a few more hours, rather than continue to get worse and deteriorate for months, and get moved from his home – he disliked change, and didn't want to be in hospital or a hospice, he wanted to be at home.

My best friend told me that not only would it be illegal, but if I did assist my own father to kill himself, I would have to live with myself knowing I had done that. He felt this would be a difficult thing to live with. I didn't really understand why this would be the case, because if it had happened it would have been the logical and right thing to do. Also, it would be what my dad wanted, so I wouldn't be doing something I felt guilty about, or needed to live with. I would have just been carrying out a solution to a problem. I would have faced any legal consequences openly and honestly and faced them accepting whatever the consequences were, knowing I did the morally and logically correct thing according to the wishes of my dad.

In the end, although my dad spoke about how he was thinking about wanting to end his life on his terms, and that he would need support with this, he never reached a point of actually wanting to follow through with this. He wanted to live and survive despite the pain, more than he wanted to die because of the pain.

Dan Jones

If I was too emotional, I don't think I would have thought so clearly about this. In writing this, I can't think what emotions someone may have about this that would impact their decision of whether they would carry out assisted suicide, but whenever the topic comes up in the media it always seems to evoke emotional responses from people for or against it. To me, I think decisions about things like this need to be made on a case-by-case basis using logic and rationality, and ensuring that you are taking the wishes of the individual into consideration, not basing the decision on what *you* want. If someone wants help to take their own life due to a situation that is temporary, that will come to an end, and their reasons are that it is so unpleasant now, but an objective observer can see that the situation isn't permanent, then this is clearly a different type of situation to someone who thinks the same, but where they have a terminal illness which is only going to get worse and lead to greater deterioration. In both cases, the person is thinking the same, but in the first case they aren't seeing beyond the current situation. There, someone taking an objective and realistic look at the situation is able to see beyond this current situation. The second person *can* look beyond the current situation, and can see that it will get worse in the future.

At the end of his life, my dad was admitted to a hospice because we could no longer provide the care he needed. He wasn't happy about this, but he had no choice. On the evening before he died, I received a phone call from the hospice to tell me that dad would likely be dead within the next 24 hours and so I should go and visit him now. As a non-driver I had no easy way to get to the hospice. I had also arranged with dad to see him in the afternoon the next day. I told the hospice nurse this. She responded telling me that if he died and I wasn't there, I would feel guilty. I explained to her that I wouldn't feel guilty because even if I did visit him, he may die after I've gone home. I couldn't guarantee that he would die while I was physically in the hospice.

The next day, I spent the day teaching a hypnotherapy training course I had been on all week. At the end of the day I turned on my mobile phone before heading over to see dad. I had a missed phone call from my brother that had just come in to tell me that our dad had just died. I telephoned him back, spoke to him, and went over to the hospice as planned.

On arrival at the hospice, they asked if I wanted to see my dad. I was aware that my brother was there and he had told me that he was sat beside dad as he fell asleep and passed away peacefully. I told the nurse that dad was dead and not going anywhere, whereas my brother was alive and probably needed my support more than my dad. She showed me through to my brother, and I spoke with him for a bit before I went in.

When I saw dad lying in the hospice bed with the soft lighting and calm music playing, I thought about how peaceful he looked. I didn't find it an upsetting experience, I didn't cry or get emotional. I gently rested my left hand on his chest and commented to him how peaceful he looked now. For months, whenever I saw him he was screaming in agony, and suffering; now, he was still and silent. I thought to myself that this was how I wanted to remember him, knowing he drifted off peacefully. I thought about how I wanted to take a photograph of dad looking so peaceful almost as something that could remind me of what he was like when he wasn't in pain and suffering – I didn't take the photograph though, because I thought people would probably not understand. I didn't want to do something that could upset my brother or my dad's friends.

When I was in the hospice, I only had tears come to my eyes when my brother or dad's friend showed tears. I never found the situation sad. There wasn't anything to be sad about. Dad was dying of cancer and suffering, and now he wasn't suffering. To me, that wasn't a sad thought. The next day, I carried on teaching my hypnotherapy training course. The students, who had travelled from various places around the world to train with me, said I could have a day off if I needed to. I hadn't even thought about taking time off. I told them that I wouldn't be taking time off; for one thing, they had paid a lot of money and travelled a long way to train with me, and to get the qualification they had to undergo a specific number of hours' training. If I missed a day I would have to somehow catch them up on that, and as they weren't local people it's not like I could call them back for an extra day at some point in the future.

To me, life went on like nothing had happened. I cried if I spoke to someone about dad and they cried, like when I told my wife, but because when things are out of sight they are out of mind (this is common among those with autism spectrum disorder), even my own father dying had little impact emotionally on me. If I was teaching hypnosis, it wasn't through a backdrop of sadness about my dad being dead; if I was working with families, or supervising staff, I was focused in the moment on those things. My mind wasn't focusing on the fact my dad was dead.

One reason many people learn mindfulness is so that they can be more present, so that they don't have a mind full of thoughts of the past or future, and so that they don't spend their time worrying. I think people with autism spectrum disorder can do part of this naturally. Many still worry about things, like whether they are doing things correctly, or reacting or responding correctly. They worry about whether they have accidentally upset people. They worry about what they are supposed to do, because change has occurred that they hadn't planned for. But generally, when they are doing something they are comfortable with doing, that is what they are focused on, so in the middle of doing something, many don't necessarily worry about other things, and they don't necessarily think about other things or people.

I feel that this trait is one that can cause the most upset to parents when they have children who respond in this way, especially when it is around death or dying, and their child or teen doesn't seem to care. I cared about my dad, and others who have died, but others may think that I am cold and uncaring because I don't think about things in the same way.

An Autistic Perspective: Death, Dying and Loss

Last summer, my granddad died. His health had started to deteriorate a number of months earlier. About a year before his death, I spoke with him about how he was of an age where he was likely to die sooner rather than later, and I asked him if I could video him playing piano. I explained that my best memories of him were of sitting down at a piano and just playing, especially playing *In The Mood*, and *Sentimental Journey*. He had also taught me to play *In The Mood* on the piano when I was about five years old.

Granddad agreed to this, so I filmed him playing piano for about 15 minutes. He liked the footage and asked for a copy, which I put onto a DVD for him. The two people within the family whom I'd looked to for how to be as a person and whom I found interesting were my uncle who did magic, and my granddad. My granddad spent his life focused on three things: cycling, accounting, and music. Although he wasn't the greatest musician, he could pick up and play a wide variety of instruments, and he enjoyed playing and creating music. I never had a chance to really learn to play musical instruments as much as I wanted to, but I was fascinated with music, and with the way granddad would seem to go into his own world while playing music. I also liked cycling, and liked listening to granddad talk about his life experiences. I have always been interested in knowledge and wanting to preserve knowledge and pass it on; like many grandparents, without prompting granddad would talk about his past experiences, and would often share tales of his past experiences that he had had with his best friend, my 'magic' uncle.

Granddad was also a cheeky man and much loved by everyone. He was always so calm and kind, as was my uncle. These were all traits I aspired to develop within myself about how I felt people should live. Unlike my uncle and dad, who died prematurely from illness caused by smoking, and my uncle, who died suddenly and unexpectedly, granddad was in his mid-80s, so it was logical to expect that he was approaching death. He didn't suffer as much as I had seen my dad suffer a couple of years earlier. He also had far more people around to help him. I visited and helped him when I could.

I was definitely closer to my granddad than I was to my dad or others who had died before. When I was told by my brother that our granddad had died, the experience was a matter-of-fact exchange, not an emotional one. As before, when my dad died, my wife was upset when I told her. She was far more upset than she was when I told her about my dad dying, and this made me cry far more. I was fine with telling her, but as soon as she cried, so did I.

I also found that I cried when I watched the video I had made of granddad playing piano. My wife and I had spoken about this because it confused me. I didn't feel sad or happy, or any emotion I could detect when I cried. Logically it didn't seem sad: the video of granddad is a happy video. But it made me cry when I watched it. I also cried at his memorial service. I didn't cry when others were sharing their memories of granddad, apart from when a note that was found that he had written knowing he was dying shortly before he died was read out:

> *"None of us know where we're going*
>
> *When it's time to say farewell*
>
> *Some say we're heading for Heaven*
>
> *While others say 'down to Hell'*
>
> *But in my view the thing that's important is the memory for those left behind*
>
> *Of someone who's tried to be helpful*
>
> *Who's tried to be loving and kind.*
>
> *I don't know where I'll be going*
>
> *But I think many loved ones are there*
>
> *And one day we'll all be together again*
>
> *To continue our Love and our Care."*

An Autistic Perspective: Death, Dying and Loss

When it was my turn to get up and speak, I had prepared to show the video of granddad playing piano, and some video I had shot of him playing flute and piccolo in his last performance with a band just two months prior to his death. I had planned to say a little about what my granddad meant to me, what my memories of him were, and what his influence had been on me. Because I knew that I was going to show the video, every time I saw this on this sheet of paper I had my notes on, I was reminded of it and would start to cry.

I think something interesting is that many people apologise when they start to cry, or they feel self-conscious. Alternatively, they simply don't do things like talking at a memorial service, because they worry that they may cry. Yet, despite people saying I must bottle my emotions up, and that I never let people know how I'm feeling, the reality is that I have no problem letting people know how I am feeling. I am honest, so if I say I don't feel anything, that is an honest answer, and when I do feel something you get the raw expression of it. I don't try to hide it. So when I cried at the memorial, I didn't try to hide it, I didn't have a problem with it, because to me that was me in that moment. I wasn't embarrassed or self-conscious; the only thing I worried about was that it was an inconvenience because I was trying to speak. I was also open with people mid-speech about why I was crying - that I knew what was coming, and whenever I watch it, it makes me cry, so thinking about it in this context was making me cry before even watching it. I cried while watching the video with the others who were present at the memorial, but as soon as the video was over I had no tears, and was back to 'normal'.

Although everyone with autism spectrum disorder is different, and so my experiences, which I've tried to share as openly and fully as possible, may not be related to by some people, I'm aware from my professional experiences and training, and from others I've met who have autism spectrum disorder, that many people do think about things in a similar way to me, but often keep that thinking to themselves because they get judged and called cold, or that they are bottling things up rather than dealing with them.

I think that those with a similar autistic perspective on death and dying can help them to be more practical when helping others, because they don't get bogged down with the emotional content of a situation. They may find uncertainty difficult to handle, and part of this can be improved by what frame of reference is being given to a situation, so you may not have certainty about when someone will die. If your focus is on that uncertainty there is no way to resolve it; you just have to accept it and cope with it. Whereas, if the focus is on 'they will be dying soon', you can be certain of this in situations where you know the person is dying.

I have had years of experience working in the caring profession, so I had certain learnt skills to know what to do once I was told what was expected of me. Others with autism may not have those skills. This can create anxiety, because they are learning something new while trying to deal with the dying or death of a loved one.

I think that the way many with autism seem to compartmentalise and think about things in a way that when something is out of sight, it is out of mind, can be protective for the wellbeing of the person with autism; however, it can make them come across as uncaring, when this isn't the case at all. Oftentimes, they just aren't thinking about that person, or their death, or dying. When they do think about the person, they may struggle with how overwhelming the emotions can be, especially if they are generally an emotional person.

I find it interesting that my own memories can trigger emotion, yet the actual situation doesn't seem to do so. This is also something I have known with many who are autistic, that they can appear cold and uncaring in a situation due to seeming unresponsive and unemotional, yet they can then create an inner experience that causes them overwhelming emotion. And once they stop thinking about this, the emotion almost instantly disappears.

I don't know why this should be the case, but I have worked with parents where they are upset in a situation, and their child or teen isn't bothered at all, and they want their child or teen to show they care, not appear ambivalent. It is almost like the external and internal are disconnected. For example, I could see my dad suffering in front of me and not feel anything, and just be practical and emotionless. I can talk about my dad suffering and unless the person I'm talking to cries, I don't feel anything. I can think about my dad suffering and this won't emotionally impact me; yet when I was writing this chapter and writing about my dad suffering, and so I was doing more than superficially thinking about him suffering, this brought tears to my eyes. As soon as I had finished writing those sections I was fine again and was thinking about the next thing.

Dan Jones

CHAPTER FIVE

Conclusion

Throughout this book, I have tried to describe in a frank and open way my experiences of loss, dying and death, to help give some insight into how someone with autism spectrum disorder processes these difficult areas of life. I wanted to show how it can be a different way of thinking and processing the world to others, and how sometimes this can be misunderstood by people trying to interpret our behaviours, thoughts and responses through their model of reality about how they think we should respond.

I have also tried to share some ideas along the way about these misunderstandings. I hope I have helped to share some insight and ideas into how someone can support the autistic person through periods of loss, or the death of loved ones.

Obviously, every autistic person is different, so no two people will have exactly the same traits or ways of processing things, but there are some similarities many people with autism share in how they process what happens around them.

Most of what I have covered in this book has been to give you as best an insight into the mind of an autistic person as possible, by sharing exactly how I process the world. In this final chapter, I want to round up with some ideas and tips around supporting those with autism spectrum disorder when they face loss or death. There are some traits that all those with autism spectrum disorder will have to some extent or another, and so how they react to loss or death will be influenced by these traits. To cover these different areas, I will break them down using the *Triad of Impairments* model, and then additional difficulties those with autism often experience.

The triad of impairments model describes three areas that autism difficulties fall into:

- Impairment in imagination;
- Impairment in social relationships; and
- Impairment in social communication.

Impairment of imagination

This can include: struggling to understand people's points of view or their feelings, difficulties handling changes to their routine or uncertainty, and taking things literally.

When it comes to loss or death, the autistic individual may struggle with understanding how others are feeling. They may not feel the same and so may say or do something that seems insensitive. If this is the case, it isn't that they are insensitive, it is just a different way of responding. It can be useful to take time to talk to them and explain how others think and feel, but it isn't helpful to try to force them to think and feel the same.

I am aware that when people die, others find this sad and may spend weeks or months mourning, but that isn't my experience. When people have tried to tell me that I should be responding a specific way, I can't somehow magically do this. What is helpful is to respect this difference, and not to see it as a problem or to treat the individual as if they are faulty in some way because they think differently.

The same applies with things like relationship breakups. The autistic individual may well continue on with their life quickly, rather than spending months being sad and mourning the end

An Autistic Perspective: Death, Dying and Loss

of the relationship. This doesn't mean they didn't care, it is just the way they are and the way they process the world. And with life transitions, like moving out of home and into independent living, or changing school: if they have left home and they never telephone or visit, it doesn't mean they don't care. These things just rarely cross their mind. They may not necessarily realise that others see their behaviour as insensitive and uncaring, and if a friend or family member gets angry with them for not keeping in touch, they are likely to be confused about why this is an issue, and not necessarily see or understand the other person's side of things.

I think one of the most important things someone can do is to accept them for who they are and how they are without making assumptions not based on facts. It isn't a fact that someone not seeing their family is insensitive and uncaring. It is only a fact that they haven't seen their family; there is no evidence for the reason for this.

If loss or death is tied to a routine, this can cause significant anxiety or anger for the autistic individual, as they struggle with the routine change and uncertainty. If the loss is expected, like with transitions from one school to another, or from one job to another, or from home to independence, then there can be a period of planning and work to build up to this so that it isn't just suddenly thrust upon the individual. Likewise, if someone is dying and the autistic person is close to that individual, or has a regular routine involving that individual, then the death is likely to bring anxiety or anger as they find themselves struggling with the sudden change in routine and uncertainty about what is happening and when, and a desire to control their environment and gain back that certainty. So, if they visit a grandparent for dinner every Sunday, and then the grandparent is dying, if this isn't prepared for it will be very difficult.

So you want to start working on what the routine will be in the future, and making sure there is a clear routine in place. Look at how and when this routine will start. Will it be transitioned in slowly? Will it be in place ready but not actually start until after that relative has died? Both of these options could lead to anxiety and anger for the autistic individual, but you would generally know what type of option would be best for that individual.

If they are moving schools, they may well need a few months of semi-regular school visits, so that by the time they are full-time in the new school they are comfortable with it. If they are transitioning from home life to independent living, then over the six months or a year or more before they move out of home, they may need to gradually take on more chores of their own: doing their own washing up, laundry, ironing, cooking, and cleaning.

Then as it gets closer to moving out, they may need to spend time away from home staying somewhere else to get used to this as an idea, and in the few months before permanently moving out there may need to be a transition and introduction to where they will be living, what the place is like, what the area is like, how they do their own things, and an introduction to doing things they never have had to do before, like the idea of paying bills, and helping them to establish the routines around these new areas. If they don't have any specific routines in relation to the death of someone, then they may well cope fine with that person's death because it doesn't really have any impact on their day-to-day life.

Impairment of social relationships

This can include: difficulties with understanding and using nonverbal behaviour, not differentiating how to behave with different people, but instead behaving the same with everybody whether friend, relative, or stranger, struggling to make and maintain friendships.

Loss can be made more difficult by struggling to understand and use non-verbal behaviour. The autistic individual may not pick up that school friends are sad about them leaving the school, or they may not pick up that family are sad about them leaving home. Many with autism don't really hug, and yet this may be what other individuals want to happen, and they may get upset or hurt because of this.

One way to be helpful is to educate them around non-verbal behaviour; in a way that they will understand, coach them about what to expect, and what may be a good way to respond. So if they are moving school, perhaps they need to have it explained to them that friends of theirs will miss them and will be sad, and may need them to say goodbye personally, and may need them to keep in touch after they have left the school.

If they leave home, maybe they need to have it explained how the parents will be feeling, and on the day, rather than just being sad and saying goodbye, perhaps telling the autistic person that you are sad so that they know, and if you would like a hug, for example, telling them that as well. It is very easy for them just to leave with their belongings and not think to say goodbye. Then, once they have left, they may not think of getting in touch, so if you want to keep the autistic person in your life you are likely to need to be the main instigator of maintaining the relationship, and are likely to need to contact them to arrange to see them.

In relation to someone dying, they may not recognise the non-verbal behaviour of others who are sad about it, so they may be carrying on as if nothing has happened, which can seem insensitive. Yet, they aren't actually doing this from a place of being insensitive. So a family member could die, and the autistic individual's mother could be sat upset on the sofa, and the autistic individual may come in demanding things, being upset that dinner isn't ready when it is supposed to be, and not picking up on the non-verbal behaviour of the mother.

So it is useful to talk openly and honestly about feelings and, at times like this, to calmly explain the situation, rather than being angry with them for their insensitivity. Most of the time, when someone with autism does something which seems inappropriate or makes someone angry, that was just an unfortunate by-product of them being themselves. It wasn't an intentional outcome of their behaviour.

Something else that is similar to this is that they may not recognise that they should behave differently with different people. So, if a granddad has died, maybe they should behave differently with grandma, and perhaps offer words of comfort, rather than treating grandma the same as they treat their friends. Or maybe they shouldn't talk about certain subjects with certain people, because those subjects upset those people. Or maybe talking about death and dying with a relative who is old and not likely to be alive much longer, or one who is sick and dying, is upsetting to those people.

These aren't thoughts that instinctively come to mind. As mentioned in the previous chapter, I openly spoke to my granddad about dying and how I wanted to video him playing piano before he died. I was very matter-of-fact about this. I didn't consider his feelings or thoughts, I just bluntly talked to him about this, as I would with anyone, and it would never be from a place of wanting to hurt or upset them. So it can be helpful to give guidance; especially if the autistic person is a child or a teenager, you can educate them about how they should communicate and what the reasons are for this.

Impairment of social communication

This can include: talking about what they are interested in regardless of the response of those they are talking to, lack of desire to communicate, communicating for their own needs rather than for general social engagement, and may say socially inappropriate comments.

As well as talking to anyone as if everyone were the same, the autistic individual may say socially inappropriate comments or exhibit socially inappropriate behaviours, like commenting at a funeral that the dead person looks peaceful and that they want to take a photograph (or even actually just taking the photograph). These behaviours could be seen as insensitive, even though this was never the intention.

As I have mentioned before, it is useful to educate them and coach them on how to respond, and on what the socially acceptable behaviour is for the situation. If it is a situation like a funeral, then there may well be a clear routine that the autistic individual can be helped to learn. Having this routine can be comforting to them, and can actually help them to say and do appropriate things, because they are comfortable to follow the routine. By educating them on what to expect, and trying to think of different observations they may make, or things they may notice and not understand, you can explain these to them upfront. So if people may cry, then they can be told that people may cry and the reasons for this; then, when they see people crying, hopefully they won't blurt out to the grieving person: 'Why are you crying?'

If they are caring for a loved one during the dying process they may have a tendency to still be largely focused on themselves when talking to the dying person, rather than recognising the need to be focusing on that person instead. If the autistic person has someone in their life supporting them, then it can be helpful for that person to help them to learn how to focus on the needs of the other person, and explain to them the importance of doing this. If the autistic person has no support and is having to care for a loved one during the end of their life, then they may need to find ways to remind themselves to keep the focus on the person they are looking after.

I have significant training as a therapist and social care worker, and yet I find it easy to slip into focusing on myself. So, even with lots of training, without constant reflection from moment to moment about what I am saying and doing, it is easy to slip into 'me, me, me' mode. I find that I can do this for the duration of therapy sessions, as I have trained to make sure that, when I am working with a client, for the duration of the session, they are the only thing I am thinking of.

In other care situations, then, I have to think about them as if they are work situations, and get in that mindset of keeping all of my focus on the person I am caring for. If I find that a sentence which is about to come out of my mouth is going to be to meet my needs and not for the benefit of the person I am focusing on, then I don't say it. This takes a lot of mental effort and focus. Up to a point, I can now do it reasonably automatically just by deciding to focus on the other person and trying to figure things out about them, but over about 90 minutes or so I start to drift back into 'normal Dan' mode.

Additional challenges

These can include: over- or under-sensitivity to sensory input – touch, taste, smells, sounds, light, visual stimuli, anxiety or anger, attention difficulties, and difficulties with keeping more than one thing in mind.

The sensory environment can play a huge role in how an autistic person handles loss, dying or death. If they transition from one school to another, or to a different job, or to a new home, then these new situations could come with new and challenging environments. Not only would there be the potential challenges of the change in routine and the uncertainty, but a new home could have noisy traffic, where the old home didn't, or the light in the rooms could be too bright or dim; or a school could be very open, where the previous school was smaller and more enclosed. Likewise, a hospital may have lots of flickering lights, and different noises, and people moving everywhere. Even something like the echo and the way the sound reverberates around a church, especially if there are lots of people in there, can cause sensory overload leading to the autistic person experiencing anger or anxiety as they feel a desire to try to escape the situation.

An Autistic Perspective: Death, Dying and Loss

It is common for those with autism to experience anger or anxiety. These are fight or flight responses. The fight or flight response is a primal response to get the individual to safety. If they feel trapped in a situation, or are experiencing physical or psychological pain, they will experience anxiety; they will first try to escape. If they can't escape the situation or pain, then they may respond with anger to fight so that they can escape the situation. Some people freeze instead of fighting or fleeing. These people may just become deeply withdrawn and unresponsive as they escape inside themselves.

The antidote to anger and anxiety is relaxation. It is useful for the autistic individual to learn meditation or a relaxation technique that they can do generally to relax - something they can do to relax when they notice themselves getting anxious or angry. It can be difficult to do a relaxation technique once you start to become angry or anxious, because it can happen so quickly.

A good technique for managing anxiety or anger when it strikes is ideally, if it is safe and appropriate to do so, to sit down. Sitting is a calming act. Let the shoulders slump, and imagine the all the muscles in the body are so heavy and relaxed that they can't move. Do 7-11 breathing. This is a breathing process where the individual breathes in counting in their mind to 7, and then out in their mind counting to 11. This longer outbreath triggers the relaxation response. So a few of these breaths can quickly help to calm someone down. A parent can teach their autistic child or teen this breathing technique and practice it with them, and if they are with the child in a situation when they feel anxious or angry, they can help the child or teen to focus on their breathing, and help to guide them to do this technique.

The autistic individual can also mentally rehearse situations. They can practice walking between lessons in a new school, or being calm and breathing in a calm way while they are supporting someone who is dying, or while attending a funeral, etc. Regular mental rehearsal is a great way for someone to prepare to handle situations. It is like exposure therapy, except that it is done in the safety and comfort of the individual's own mind until they have mastered what they are rehearsing.

They could mentally rehearse how they will handle their last day of school, or a new routine, and how they will make sure that goes well. Likewise for leaving home, or moving into a new home, or leaving a job, or supporting a dying loved one, or responding in a specific way when a loved one dies.

Another consideration for relaxation or for bringing down anger or anxiety levels is to reduce sensory input. This could be by 'stimming', where the autistic individual may stroke, or tap, or hum or whistle, or do some self-stimulating process that helps them to become absorbed in that and to relax. It could be by using headphones to shut out excessive noise, or sunglasses to shut out bright light and reduce the input from all of the movement. It could be to have an area of the environment which is lower in sensory input. So, for example, I try to sit in cafés or restaurants in a corner where I can face a wall or look out of a window to a calming open scene, and in workplaces I like to be at a desk with high desk dividers with nothing on them so that they are just a plain colour, then I can look at this to reduce sensory input. I also focus inwardly, almost like meditating, so that my eyes are defocused and I'm not paying attention externally, and I focus on my inner world and on breathing.

The autistic individual may have difficulties with attention, or with keeping things in their mind. It is interesting that many autistic individuals can focus their attention on one topic for an extended period of time, but in other contexts find that they are easily distracted, especially by lots of sensory input. If they are caring for someone who is dying then this can be a challenge, because they may regularly forget what they have been asked to do. They will also need clear and detailed instructions to follow, rather than working on their own initiative. It is common for them to remember just the last little bit that they heard when they are spoken to, and if this isn't clear (for example, if it was spoken in vague language or metaphors) then they will remember even less, and what they do remember they may well not fully understand and so may make mistakes.

If the person is in a hospital or a high-sensory environment, then this may make it even more challenging for the autistic individual. They may easily get lost in corridors, and may well struggle to hold their attention on anything. To help them hold their attention it is helpful to have clear and concise instructions, and just a few steps listed at a time. Don't rely on verbal instructions alone. These are easy to forget. It is best to have things written down. Encourage them to feed back what they have done, and even ask them to explain what they have been asked to do.

It could be that they are an adult with autism who doesn't have someone to support them. In which case, they can write lists and ask for advice, but they will have to remember to do this for themselves. When supporting someone with autism spectrum disorder, it isn't about trying to make them join you in your model of the world, and how you process things, but about helping them from within their model of the world and from how they naturally process things. Autistic individuals process the world differently, but the way they process the world is right for them.

An Autistic Perspective: Death, Dying and Loss